Although it gives little idea of the actual sound, the following is the specification of the organ completed in 1724 by the firm of Renatus Harris for St. Dionis Backchurch, Fenchurch Street, London. This church, which was rebuilt after the Great Fire of 1666 from the designs of Sir Christopher Wren, was demolished in 1879. John Bennett was organist from 1752 until 1784, having succeeded Charles Burney.

Great (*GG to D*)
Open Diapason 8
Stopped Diapason 8
Principal 4
Twelfth 2⅔ Fifteenth 2 (one stop)
Tierce 1⅗
Larigot 1⅓
Sesquialtera (4 ranks)
Cornet (from middle C up) (5 ranks)
Trumpet 8
French Horn (from Tenor D up) 8
Clarion 4
Cremona 8 (from Choir)

Swell (*from fiddle G*)
Open Diapason 8
Stopped Diapason 8
Cornet (4 ranks)
Trumpet 8
Clarion 4
Cremona 8
Vox Humana 8

Choir
Open Diapason 8
Stopped Diapason 8
Principal 4
Flute 4
Bassoon
Cremona 8
Clarion 4 (from Great)
Vox Humana 8

Book 4
Contents

Preface

In choice of stops the aim should be clarity, particularly in the louder pieces. Although changes of manual are sometimes indicated, all the pieces in this book can be played effectively on a one-manual organ.

In the original editions there are frequently no directions either for registration or tempo. Apart from which manual to be used [e.g. Great, Swell, Chair (sometimes Chaire or Chayre) i.e. the equivalent of the German *Rückpositiv*—the *positiv* organ at the back of the player], the usual directions are Trumpet, Cornet, Vox Humana, Flute, Diapasons, Eccho, Soft Organ, Loud, and Full Organ—the latter being the full organ of the composer's time. Full Organ is probably best realised by the following:

Gt. light Diapasons 8.4. (2⅔.) 2. Mixture.

or Gt. light Diapasons 8.4. (2.) coupled to Sw. Diapasons 8.4.2. Mixture. (box open)

If harsh or strident, the Mixture should not be used in either case.

Following are suggestions for registration with equivalents:

Gt. light Diapasons 8.4. (2.) – Small Open Diapason (or Flute) 8. Principal 4. (Fifteenth 2.)

Gt. light 8.4.2. – Flutes 8.4. Fifteenth 2.

Gt. light 8.2. – Small Open Diapason (or Flute) 8. Fifteenth 2.

Light 8.4. – Gt. Flute (or Dulciana) 8. Flute 4. [or Ch. Flutes 8.4.]

In most cases Stopped Diapason 8. is probably better than Flute 8. The large Open Diapason 8. should *not* be used.

Cornet Voluntaries. If there is no Cornet, the following alternatives are suggested:

{ R.H. Gt. light 8.4.2. (or 8.2.)
  L.H. Sw. 8.4. (2.) [Sw. to Gt.?]

or { R.H. Sw. Oboe 8. [or 8 ft. stop(s)]. Fifteenth 2. (Mixture.)
     L.H. Ch. 8.4. (2.) [or Gt. soft 8. (4.)]

or Gt. (or Sw. or Ch.) 8.4.2. both hands

In the latter case and if the organ is a one-manual, for the echo or dialogue effects, a stop (2 ft.?) could be withdrawn or the passage phrased differently e.g. *staccato*.

Trumpet Voluntaries. The Tuba should *not* be used. If there is no Trumpet, the following alternatives are suggested:

{ R.H. Gt. Diapason(s) 8. (4.)
  L.H. Sw. 8.4. (2.) [Sw. to Gt.?]

or Gt. light Diapason(s) (2.) 8.4. (2.) both hands

In the latter case and if the organ is a one-manual, the echo or dialogue effects could be played as suggested in the Cornet Voluntaries.

Stops with the same names do not always produce the same effect on different organs. Players should use other registrations if those suggested are not effective or suitable on any particular instrument.

The directions for registration which are enclosed in brackets may be used or not at the player's discretion.

The tempo indications are the composer's except those enclosed in brackets which are the editor's.

C.H.T

Vorwort

Für den Fall, dass mehrere Register zur Wahl stehen, empfiehlt es sich, insbesonders auf die Reinheit des Klanges zu achten. Dies gilt speziell für Stücke mit grösserem Tonvolumen. Obwohl in den vorliegenden Werken in einigen Fällen Manualwechsel angegeben sind, können alle Kompositionen jedoch auch ohne weiteres auf einer Orgel mit nur einem Manual gespielt werden.

Vielfach sind in den Originalausgaben keinerlei Anweisungen für Registratur oder Tempo vorhanden. Neben den Angaben bezüglich der Wahl des Manuals (z.B. Great, Swell, Chair—manchmal auch Chaire oder Chayre, und gleichbedeutend mit dem Deutschen 'Rückpositiv') sind die gebräuchlichsten Bezeichnungen Trumpet, Cornet, Vox Humana, Flute, Diapasons, Eccho, Soft Organ, Loud Organ und Full Organ—letztere das Volle Werk einer zur Entstehungszeit gebräuchlichen Orgel bezeichnend.

Volles Werk [Full Organ] lässt sich am besten folgendermassen erzielen:

I kleine Prinzipalen 8'.4'. (2⅔'.) 2'. Mixtur. [Gt. light Diapasons 8.4. (2⅔.) 2. Mixture.] oder I kleine Prinzipalen 8'.4'. (2'.) nebst Koppel zu III Prinzipalen 8'.4'.2'. Mixtur. (Schweller offen). [Gt. light Diapasons 8.4. (2.) coupled to Sw. Diapasons 8.4.2. Mixture. (box open)]

Sollte die Mixtur einen schrillen oder grellen Ton ergeben, wird empfohlen, sie in beiden Fällen *nicht* zu verwenden.

Nachstehend Beispiele einiger Registratur-Vorschläge, und ihre Bedeutungen:

Gt. light Diapasons 8.4. (2.) – Gemshorn (oder Spitzflöte) 8'. Oktave 4'. (Superoktave 2'.)

Gt. light 8.4.2. – I Flöten 8'.4'. Superoktave 2'.

Gt. light 8.2 – I Gemshorn (oder Spitzflöte oder Flöte) 8'. Superoktave 2'.

Light 8.4. – I oder II oder III Flöten 8'.4'.

Das Grosse Prinzipal 8'. ist in *keinem* dieser Fälle zu verwenden.

Cornet Voluntaries. Sollte an der Orgel kein Kornett vorhanden sein, können folgende Alternativen verwendet werden:

{ R.H. I Gemshorn (oder Spitzflöte 8'. (Oktave 4'.) Superoktave 2'.
  L.H. III 8'.4'. (2'.) [I + III?]

oder { R.H. III Oboe (oder Prinzipal) 8'. Superoktave 2'. (Mixtur.)
       L.H. II 8'.4'. (2'.) [oder I sanft 8'. (4'.)]

oder I (oder II oder III) 8'.4'.2'. beide Hände.

Für das letzte Beispiel, und für den Fall, dass die Orgel nur ein Manual aufweist, kann für die Echo- und Dialogeffekte entweder ein Register (2'?) eingezogen werden, oder man kann auch den Lauf etwas anders phrasieren, etwa *staccato*.

Trumpet Voluntaries. Die Hochdrucktuba ist hier *nicht* zu verwenden. Für den Fall, dass keine Trompete vorhanden ist, können folgende Alternativen verwendet werden:

{ R.H. I Prinzipale 8'. (4'.)
  L.H. III 8'.4'. (2'.) [I + III?]

oder I Gemshorn (oder Spitzflöte) 8'. Oktave 4'. (Superoktave 2'.) beide Hände.

Im letzteren Falle, und auch wenn die Orgel nur ein Manual hat, können die Echo- und Dialogeffekte entsprechend den Vorschlägen unter 'Cornet Voluntaries' gespielt werden.

Es ist zu beachten, dass trotz gleichlautender Bezeichnungen die Register der verschiedenen Orgeln nicht immer den gleichen klanglichen Effekt ergeben. Es empfiehlt sich daher, andere Register zu verwenden, sollten sich die im Werk vorgeschlagenen als ungeeignet erweisen.

Die Registeranweisungen in Klammern sind nicht bindend. Die angegebenen Spielgeschwindigkeiten sind bis auf die vom Herausgeber in Klammern hinzugefügten Bemerkungen die Originalangaben des Komponisten.

C.H.T

OLD ENGLISH ORGAN MUSIC

Edited by C. H. TREVOR

Book IV

DIAPASON MOVEMENT

(from a voluntary)

Sw. (or Gt.) Diapason 8.

John Bennett (1735-1784)

Adagio

Printed in Great Britain

OXFORD UNIVERSITY PRESS, MUSIC DEPARTMENT, GREAT CLARENDON STREET, OXFORD OX2 6DP

4

VOLUNTARY IN G

Largo Gt. light Diapasons 8. 4. (2.)
Moderato Gt. light Diapasons 8. 4. (2.)
Sw. 8. 4. 2. (Mixture.) box closed
Sw. to Gt.

William Boyce (1710-1779)

The composer's registration: Full Organ (see preface)

The *poco a poco cresc.* should be made by gradually opening the swell box. The new "swelling organ", as it was called, was introduced in 1712 by Abraham Jordan at the church of St. Magnus the Martyr, London Bridge. In his "Present state of music in France and Italy", Burney complains of finding no swell organs in 1770. Three stops were placed in a swell-box in the organ of St. Michael's Church, Hamburg, but with so little effect that Burney, who heard the organ in 1762, says that if he had not been told there was a swell he would not have noticed it.

ADAGIO
(from a voluntary)

John Travers (1703-1758)

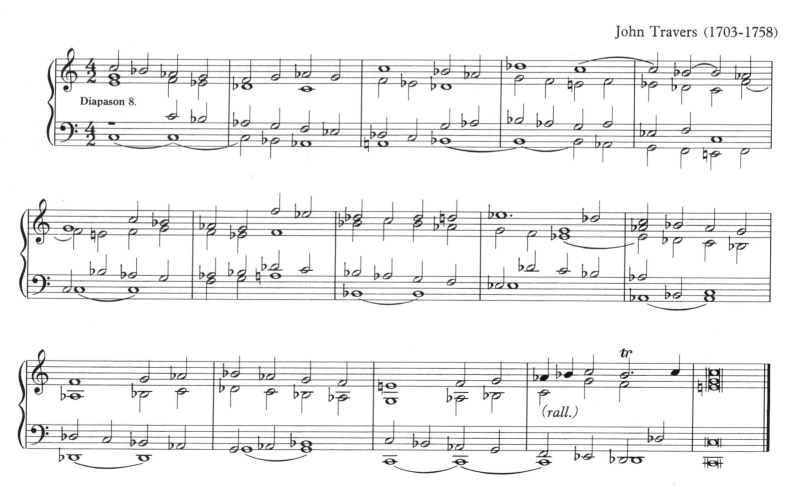

SICILIANO
(from a voluntary)

John Stanley (1713-1786)

Sw. Diapason 8.

(rall.)

VOLUNTARY IN B FLAT

Maurice Greene (1695-1755)

9

Old English Organ Music for Manuals (Vol. IV)

SHORT VOLUNTARY

Full Organ (see preface)

John Worgan (1724-1790)

DIAPASON MOVEMENT
(from a voluntary)

William Walond (1725-1770)

Diapason 8.

FUGHETTA IN A

Charles Burney (1726–1814)

TRUMPET VOLUNTARY

Henry Heron (18th century)

★See preface for alternative registrations.

(allargando)

TWO PIECES

No. 1 AIR

Samuel Wesley (1766-1837)

The registration is the composer's. The piece can be played throughout with both hands on soft Flute(s) 8. (4.)

No. 2 GAVOTTE

light Flutes 8. 4. (2.)

The composer's registration: Diapasons with Principal. The composer's indicated *tempo* seems excessive and may be a misprint for ♩ = 104. This however seems to be too slow. Probably ♩ = 120 is appropriate.

CORNET VOLUNTARY

*R.H. Cornet (8. 4. 2⅔. 2. 1⅗.)
L.H. 8. 4. (2.)

Starling Goodwin (18th century)

*See preface for alternative registrations.

Old English Organ Music for Manuals (Vol. IV)

THREE INTERLUDES

John Travers (1703–1758)

VOLUNTARY IN F

William Hine (1687–1730)

Continued overleaf

Old English Organ Music for Manuals (Vol. IV)

DIAPASON MOVEMENT
(from a voluntary)

Gt. light Diapason(s) 8. (4.)

John Stanley (1713-1786)

Processed and printed by
Halstan & Co. Ltd., Amersham, Bucks., England

OXFORD UNIVERSITY PRESS